The Ultimate
STUFFED
BURGER
PRESS

Hamburger Patty Maker Recipe Book

CLOSE

Rex Houston

LEGAL

NOTE: Some of the recipes in this book include raw eggs. Raw eggs may contain bacteria. It is recommended that you purchase certified salmonella-free eggs from a reliable source and store them in the refrigerator. You should not feed raw eggs to babies or small kids. Likewise, pregnant women, elderly persons, or those with a compromised immune system should not eat raw eggs. Neither the author nor the publisher claims responsibility for adverse effects resulting from the use of the recipes and/or information found within this book.

INTRODUCTION

FINGER LICKIN' DELICIOUSNESS!

IT'S LIKE A CULINARY EXPLOSION IN YOUR MOUTH!

Going out for Burgers just won't be the same anymore! Be the master of your domain and get grilling! Jam that meat with anything you want! Be your own creator of Blissful Deliciousness. The mouths you feed will appreciate the desirable Gourmet Burgers that are going on that grill! Pure heaven after a simple bite and your bragging rights are open for business! Make sure that you are creative and "Get Jiggy with It" between the bun! We have some very special recipes for you with some of the most, catchy names in the business for you to enjoy, but we want you to come up with your very own creativity. So, we added a section in the back of the book where you can log your progress, as you explore and come up with your very own menu of choice. You will be at awe after using this skillet or grilling tool to make your burgers. Let us know what masterpiece you come up with, or create next. You never know...your recipe may just be a part of our next series of this book. From your Friendly, Neighborhood Burger Team! Enjoy...

TABLE OF CONTENTS

CHAPTER 1:
EVERYONE LOVES BURGERS!

THEY'RE SO DELICIOUS

Who doesn't love a good burger? As a kid growing up there was nothing better than a hamburger and fries for lunch or dinner. The juicy meat, the melted cheese, a toasted bun, and all my favorite condiments. The flavors just go so well together. It's a comfort food for so many. I can't think of a better way to cheer up than a bite of a tasty burger.

You can have fun eating them with your hands and they don't create a mess... unless you want them to. You can eat them on the go, or just about anywhere you'd like. And they're the perfect food for any occasion.

It's one of the most American foods out there along with apple pie. People have been eating hamburgers in the US since 1895. It's woven into the fabric of our culture and is beloved by all different types of people.

The best part of a burger is they're totally customizable. Burger joints are popping up all over the country that let you choose all sorts of crazy condiments. It's one of those foods that allows you to make it your way. Have fun and get creative with your burger! Let it show off your style!

CHAPTER 2:
WHY A BURGER PRESS?

THE FLAVOR SECRET

Everyone wants flavor in their burger. It's one of the things that makes burger so great. The burger press allows you to maximize flavor by putting condiments in the middle of your burger.

Imagine biting into a juicy hamburger and getting some melted cheesy goodness along with some bacon. That will wake up your taste buds in the best way possible. When you stuff your burgers you get punched in the mouth flavor with every bite. It's like the ultimate burger. Just think about how great it is to have melted cheese ooze out of your burger instead of sitting on top of it.

You can play around with different flavor combinations and keep it all a secret until that first bite. There's nothing better biting into a burger and getting the heat from some unknown jalapeños in there. Your mouth will be headed straight to flavor town.

When you stuff a burger, you cook the flavors into every bite. You're never going to want a normal hamburger again after you've savored the flavor of a stuffed burger.

IMPRESS YOUR FRIENDS AND FAMILY

When you cook your loved ones you want them to say **"Wow That Was Amazing"**. The burger press does that every single time. Imagine their faces when they discover there's cheese in the middle of their burger. Everyone will think you're some kind of cooking magician. They'll wonder how you got toppings so perfectly in the middle of the burger.

You can pretend like you slaved away and spent extra time getting those toppings so perfectly in the middle of your burger. Secretly you'll know how easy it was for you to do it with the burger press. Taking all the praise without spending any extra time making your burgers.

Take pride in knowing that your family is eating food they love and you made it. There is no better feeling than seeing a smile on your love ones face as they eat the food you cooked. Be careful though, your friends and family may start coming over for dinner all the time once you start eating your burgers.

CHAPTER 3: PRESSED PERFECTION!

THE PERFECT LOOKING PATTY

Do you struggle to form good patties? Well you can kiss those days away with a burger press. The burger press creates a perfect looking 4 ounce patty every single time. Once you stick your ground meat into the press it does all the work with a little help from you. You got a put in a little work, right?

Once you take the patty out of the press it will be perfectly rounded and nice and thick. It will look like it came out of a fancy restaurant. The press will always maintain its shape and allow you to easily trim off any extra meat so that all of your patties are identical and eye catching.

The patties are so well form when they come out of the press that you don't have to worry about them falling apart. You'll never have another burger fall apart on the grill or stuffed toppings fall out while cooking.

SLIDERS "R" US!

Sliders are great hors d'oeuvre and party food. They're especially good for young children that can't eat an entire burger. The one problem is they can be hard to make. Making good regular sized patties is hard enough, let alone making them smaller. You want them to be a miniature version of perfect burger patties. All you need is your burger press and you're good to go.

Your burger press comes with a special piece so that you can make sliders. You'll never have to worry about creating those little patties ever again. Your grill press will get it done for you in seconds, so that you can make all the sliders you need for your next event.

CHAPTER 4:
GRILL, FRY, OR BAKE'EM
LIKE A CHAMP!

THE CHOICE IS YOURS

You've got options when comes to cooking your burgers. They all will make your burger taste different. Some of it will also depend on what you have on hand. Not everyone has access to a grill, but most people will have access to a stove top or oven.

Grilling them is the classic way to do it. You end up with those nice char marks from the grill on the burger. Grilling them adds a nice smoky flavor to the meat. Make sure you don't pat the burgers down with any of your utensils. Pushing the burgers down twill release the juices.

Frying them on the stove top will make a diner style burger. This is especially true yes you use a cast-iron skillet. Just like with grilling make sure you don't push down on the burgers and release the juices. Use meat with a higher fat content when frying because you lose more fat when you fry the meat.

Cooking burgers in the oven is another option. Cooking your burger in the oven leads to a juicy burger because heat is distributed evenly in an oven and you can control the exact temperature. Always make sure you place something under the meat to catch the drippings. You can broil them in the oven to mimic grilling if you don't own a grill.

In addition to ingredients and preparation, you must also be precise with your cooking. Different meats require different times on the grill or pan, and eaters have different tastes and styles they prefer. Here is a small table for reference:

CHAPTER 5:
THE BUN, THE WHOLE BUN, AND NOTHING BUT THE BUN!

THINK BETWEEN THE BUN

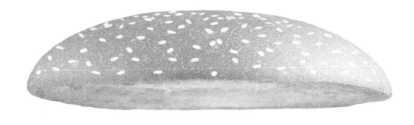

Hamburger buns are the lease thought about part of a burger. There are so many different things you can do with the bun. You can use pretzel bread, whole wheat, onion buns, and a whole lot more. If you're trying to avoid carbs you can always wrap your burger and lettuce and eat a protein style. If you really want to go over the top slap your burger between two big chunks of Ramen noodles. That's a burger you wall soon forget.

If you decide to go with bread or a bun make sure you give it some love. Slather the cut side with a little melted butter and toasted in a sauté pan or on the grill. You put effort to every other part of the burger why not finish it off with the bun? A toasted bun adds nice texture and the butter adds delicious flavor.

At the end of the day you can use anything as long as your burger will fit inside of it. Get creative and have some fun with your buns!

CHAPTER 6:
DRESS IT UP!

GET CREATIVE WITH YOU CONDIMENTS!

If you really want impress your friends, family, and taste buds get creative with the condiments. Try using arugula or watercress instead of lettuce, because they always have more flavor. Use grain mustard or Dijon mustard instead of yellow mustard too add depth to your burger. Try salsa instead of ketchup to add texture and more complex flavor. Sweeten things up with some fruit like pineapple or mango on your burger. And of course, don't forget about things like bacon, prosciutto, salami or even onion rings for extra meaty deliciousness. If you can find it in the kitchen you can put on your burger. So, let your creative juices flow one topping your burger.

CHAPTER 6: SIMPLE STEPS!

HOW TO USE YOUR BURGER PRESS

Make a burger patty with your burger press is actually quite simple. You can have your patties ready in a heartbeat with three easy steps! Once you choose your delicious ingredients it's time to make some epic burgers!

1) Get your meat ready by dividing into equal portions and rounding them into balls. Make sure you don't make them bigger than a ½ pound. Next separate each ball into a larger piece and a slightly smaller one; ideally about 60%/40% big too small.

2) Put the bigger piece of meat into the base of your Burger Press with the base plate in place. Then, take off the bottom cap from the top lid to open up the cavity creator. Push down on the meat creating a perfectly round and deep indentation directly in the middle, and then place the ingredients of your choice in the indentation.

3) Put the smaller piece of meat on top. Seal the burger, securing the ingredients in the center. Re-cap the top lid to make a flat base. Cover and push down. Always trim off any excess meat that is left around the rim. Take off the lid and, release the patty by pushing on the bottom tray. Put the patty on a clean plate for seasoning then it's off to the grill, oven, or pan and finally into your belly!

CHARTS FOR HOME COOKING

FOOD TEMPERATURES FOR SAFE HEATING, DANGER CHILLING & FREEZING ZONES!

A guide for food temperature cooking!

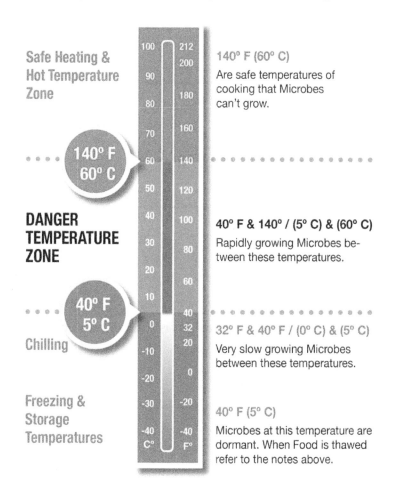

Safe Heating & Hot Temperature Zone

140° F (60° C)

Are safe temperatures of cooking that Microbes can't grow.

140° F 60° C

DANGER TEMPERATURE ZONE

40° F & 140° / (5° C) & (60° C)

Rapidly growing Microbes between these temperatures.

40° F 5° C

Chilling

32° F & 40° F / (0° C) & (5° C)

Very slow growing Microbes between these temperatures.

Freezing & Storage Temperatures

40° F (5° C)

Microbes at this temperature are dormant. When Food is thawed refer to the notes above.

COOKING CHART FOR BEEF, LAMB, CHICKEN & PORK

DONENESS	BEEF & LAMB	POULTRY	PORK
Rare (Cool Red Center)	125º Degrees	n/a	n/a
Medium Rare (Warm Red Center)	130º - 135º Degrees	n/a	145º Degrees
Medium (Warm Pink Center)	135º - 140º Degrees	n/a	150º Degrees
Medium Well (Slightly Pink Center)	140º - 150º Degrees	n/a	155º Degrees
Well Done (Little or no Pink)	155º+ Degrees	165º -175º Degrees	160º Degrees

Make sure not to undercook or overcook your meat! Do not make your burgers too moist or too dry. **Preciseness is the key to being a burger pro.**

BEFORE YOU GO ANY FURTHER!

12 Steps to Making the Perfect Stuffed or Unstuffed Burgers with your STUFFED Burger Press! This quick start guide will show you the way to get the **BEST Burgers made fast!** This **QUICK STEP GUIDE** will make you a pro at stuffing those burgers! Simply click the button below! Enjoy your Monster Burgers! GET YOURS NOW!

http://eepurl.com/dt_9IX

CHAPTER 7:

THESE BURGERS ARE NOT FOR THE WEAK!

Get ready for some jam packed, kick ass, throw down, everything you've ever wanted in a stuffed burger to impress not only your friends and family, but even impress yourself. We have put together some of the meanest, leanest mouth-watering burgers you've ever seen. These burgers are not for the weak...so I guess we will see if you can handle it! Let us know if you can!

THE EL NIÑO

This burger isn't for the weak of heart. It adds a little punch and crunch to your palate; making you going back for more. Keep this recipe close because it's gonna be a hit at the table.

Prep Time: 5 Minutes
Cook Time: 20 Minutes
Servings: 3

INGREDIENTS:
1 pound ground buffalo
2 teaspoons taco seasoning
1/3 cup salsa
¼ cup guacamole
¼ cup sour cream
3 slices jalapeno jack cheese
3 diced habaneros
Lettuce, shredded
1 diced tomato
12-14 French fried onion rings. Any will do.
3 hamburger buns

DIRECTIONS:
> Combine the ground buffalo, taco seasoning and salsa together in a bowl.

> Mix the sour cream and guacamole together in a separate bowl and set to the side.

> Form the ground buffalo mixture into 6 equal sized balls. Turn each ball into a patty by using the STUFF side of the burger press to push it down.

> Fill half of the patties with a slice of cheese and 1 piece of ham.

> Place the other patty on top of the stuffed patty.

> Use the SEAL side of the Burger Press to keep the two patties in place. Close the press firmly, which will seal the patties together. Release the press.

> Put the patties on the grill and cook for 6 minutes on each side. Place the cheese on the burger and grill for an additional 2 minutes until cheese is melted.

> Serve on a bun with habaneros, diced tomatoes, French fried onions and shredded lettuce.

THE BEEFED UP BURGER

Doubling up the patties gives you all the beef you can handle. Mixing it with the classic burger condiments will bring you back to your childhood.

Prep Time: 5 Minutes

Cook Time: 20 Minutes

Servings: 1

INGREDIENTS:

1 tablespoon finely chopped onion

1 tablespoon ketchup

1 teaspoon prepared mustard

1/4 teaspoon salt

1/8 teaspoon pepper

1 pound lean ground beef (90% lean)

1/4 cup finely shredded cheddar cheese

1 hamburger bun split

Lettuce leaves and tomato slices, optional

DIRECTIONS:

❯ Combine the onion, ketchup, mustard, salt and pepper in a bowl. Mix these ingredients with the beef.

❯ Form the ground beef mixture into four 4 ounce balls. Turn each ball into a patty by using the STUFF side of the burger press to push it down.

> Fill half of the patties with a handful of cheese in the center of the burger patty.
> Place the other patty on top of the stuffed patty..
> Use the SEAL side of the Burger Press to keep the two patties in place. Close the press firmly, which will seal the patties together. Release the press.
> Place onions in a pan and cook for 4 minutes with olive oil and the rest of the salt and pepper.
> Put the patties on the grill and cook for 6 minutes on each side.
> Serve: on a bun with lettuce and tomato if desired.

THE ARTERY CLOGGER

This is the monster burger of all burgers. Layered with two grilled cheese sandwiches and topped with onion rings, this burger will be a towering, mess of cheesy goodness.

Prep Time: 5 Minutes

Cook Time: 1 Hour

Servings: 4

INGREDIENTS:

1 pound ground beef

1 cup mushrooms, sliced

8 frozen onion rings, thawed

12 slices of cheddar cheese

4 slices of Swiss cheese

16 slices of Texas Toast

Iceberg lettuce

Secret Sauce

Secret Sauce:

½ cup Ketchup

½ cup mayonnaise

1 dill pickle, diced

DIRECTIONS:

❯ Prepare onion rings to package directions.

> Fry bacon in a pan until it is done to your liking.
> Prepare 8 grilled cheese sandwiches with one set of cheddar cheese in each.
> Combine all secret sauce ingredients.
> Sauté mushrooms in butter until brown.
> Form the burger mixture into four 4 ounce balls. Turn each ball into a patty by using the STUFF side of the burger press to push it down.
> Grill burgers for 6 minutes on each side
> Serve: grilled cheese sandwich, burger patty, one slice of cheddar and Swiss cheese, 2 slices of bacon, sautéed mushrooms, 2 onions rings, secret sauce, lettuce and top with remaining grilled cheese sandwich.

NOTHING BUT THE BEEF

The sourdough really lets the taste of the beef shine through. Cheddar in the middle complements the taste of the meat.

Prep Time: 5 Minutes

Cook Time: 17 Minutes

Servings: 4

INGREDIENTS:

1 ½ pounds lean ground beef

¾ teaspoon plus 1/8 teaspoon salt

¼ teaspoon plus 1/8 teaspoon black pepper

2 ounces cheddar cheese

4 red onion slices

2 tablespoons extra virgin olive oil

4 crusty sourdough bread slices

4 teaspoons course-grained Dijon mustard

12 plum tomato slices

DIRECTIONS:

> Combine the ground beef and ¾ teaspoon salt and ¼ teaspoon pepper into a bowl.

> Form the ground beef mixture into eight 4 ounce balls. Turn each ball into a patty by using the STUFF side of the burger press to push it down.

> Fill half of the patties with a slice of cheddar cheese in the center of each patty.
> Place the other patty on top of the stuffed patty.
> Use the SEAL side of the Burger Press to keep the two patties in place. Close the press firmly, which will seal the patties together. Release the press.
> Place onions in a pan and cook for 4 minutes with olive oil and the rest of the salt and pepper.
> Put the patties on the grill and cook for 6 minutes on each side.
> Serve on a bun and top with spread the Dijon mustard. Top with an onion and tomato on top of the burger patty.

MUSTARD GLAZED "KNOCK OUT" BURGER

The Mustard Glazed Burger pairs the spiciness of the grain mustard and compliments it with the dill pickle, flavors that will have you asking why you never glazed your burgers before.

Prep Time: 5 Minutes

Cook Time: 20 Minutes

Servings: 4

INGREDIENTS:

1½ lbs. lean ground beef

Kosher Salt

Fresh Ground Pepper

½ cup grain Mustard

1 teaspoon garlic powder

4 slices of Pepper Jack Cheese

16 dill pickle chips

DIRECTIONS:

> Mix the ground buffalo, salt, pepper, ¼ Dijon Mustard sauce, and garlic powder into a bowl.
> Form the ground buffalo into eight 4 ounce balls. Turn each ball into a patty by using the STUFF side of the burger press to push it down.
> Fill half of the patties with 4 dill pickle chips and one piece of cheese.
> Place the other patty on top of the stuffed patty.

> Use the SEAL side of the Burger Press to keep the two patties in place. Close the press firmly, which will seal the patties together. Release the press.
> Brush the patties with grain mustard on both sides
> Put the patties on the grill and cook for 6 minutes on each side. Put some more of the mustard on the patties before they are done cooking.
> Serve: Put the remaining grain mustard on a roll and top with lettuce and tomato.

COMPLETELY COMATOSED

This is the burger to top all burgers. What better than a sweet creamy donut as a bun. The sweetness of the bun is the perfect addition to brunch with the ladies, especially when you want to provide more than just coffee and donuts.

Prep Time: 5 Minutes
Cook Time: 20 Minutes
Servings: 3

INGREDIENTS:
¾ pound ground beef
3 tbsp. parsley, chopped
2 tbsp. onion, grated
House seasoning
2 tbsp. butter
3 eggs
6 slices bacon, cooked
6 glazed donuts

House seasoning:
1 cup salt
¼ cup black pepper
¼ cup garlic powder

DIRECTIONS:

> Combine the meat, parsley and onion together.

> Form the mixture into three 4 ounce balls. Turn each ball into a patty by using the STUFF side of the burger press to push it down.

> Cook burgers on grill for 6 minutes on each side

> Fry bacon in a pan until cooked to your liking

> Cook eggs on a pan or grill, adding butter so they do not stick. Cook until the yolks are set.

> Place patties on donuts; top each with 2 pieces of bacon and an egg.

> Serve with coffee or juice.

FOR THE LOVE OF BISON

The Tarragon pairs perfectly with the bison and allows it shine. We keep the ingredients to a minimum so the bison takes center stage.

Prep Time: 5 Minutes

Cook Time: 30 Minutes

Servings: 4

INGREDIENTS:
2 pounds lean ground bison

1 teaspoon dried tarragon

1/4 cup chopped parsley

salt and pepper to taste

3/4 cup blue cheese, crumbled

DIRECTIONS:
> Place the onions and mushrooms in a pan and cook for 20 minutes. Add the parsley and set to the side to cool.
> Combine the bison, parsley and tarragon in a bowl.
> Form the ground bison mixture into eight 4 ounce balls. Turn each ball into a patty by using the STUFF side of the burger press to push it down.
> Fill half of the patties with 2 tbsp. of cheese in the center of each patty.
> Place the other patty on top of the stuffed patty..

> Use the SEAL side of the Burger Press to keep the two patties in place. Close the press firmly, which will seal the patties together. Release the press.
> Place onions in a pan and cook for 4 minutes with olive oil and the rest of the salt and pepper.
> Put the patties on the grill and cook for 6 minutes on each side.
> Serve with cheese and tomato slices.

THE MARIA BURGER

If you are a tomato lover then this is the burger for you. This fresh herb piece of meat will bring your summer to life.

Prep Time: 5 Minutes

Cook Time: 20 Minutes

Servings: 6

INGREDIENTS:

3 pounds ground chuck

5 tablespoons sun-dried tomato paste

Kosher Salt

4 ounces crumbled goat cheese

3 minced garlic cloves

3 tablespoons torn fresh basil

2 teaspoons garlic salt

12 whole sun-dried tomatoes packed in oil, chopped in half

6 slices of goat cheese

6 Kaiser Rolls

½ cup mayonnaise

24 large fresh basil leaves

DIRECTIONS:

›   Mix first seven ingredients into a bowl.

›   Form the ground chuck into twelve 4 ounce balls. Turn each ball into a patty by using the STUFF side of the burger press to push it down.

> ❯ Fill half of the patties with 2 whole sun-dried tomatoes and 1 slice of goat cheeses.
> ❯ Place the other patty on top of the stuffed patty.
> ❯ Use the SEAL side of the Burger Press to keep the two patties in place. Close the press firmly, which will seal the patties together. Release the press.
> ❯ Put the patties on the grill and cook for 6 minutes on each side
> ❯ Grill over medium heat for 6 minutes on each side.
> ❯ Spread mayonnaise on a roll and garnish with 2 basil leaves on the top and bottom of the burger and then applying the bun.

THE GREEN MACHINE

This recipe is packed with a ton of flavor and on a warm summer day you can choose to ditch the bun and eat on top of a bed of lettuce instead. It's your choice. Why not make it a good one?

Prep Time: 5 Minutes

Cook Time: 20 Minutes

Servings: 6

INGREDIENTS:

Burger : 3 lbs. lean ground turkey

3 green onions, finely chopped

2 cloves garlic, minced

2 tablespoons fresh parsley, finely chopped

1 tablespoon fresh sage, finely chopped

2 tablespoons Dijon mustard

2 large eggs

¼ cup almond flour

1 teaspoon salt

½ teaspoon ground white pepper

1 ½ ripe avocado, sliced

Spicy Mayo: ¼ cup paleo mayo

¼ teaspoon garlic powder

Pinch salt

½ chipotle powder

Leftover avocado slices from burgers

Arugula

Romaine

Kale

DIRECTIONS:

> Burgers: Combine all burger ingredients, but not avocado, kale, arugula, and romaine into a bowl.

> Cut the avocados in half and slice into three slices. Toss the remaining parts of the avocado into another bowl.

> Form the mixture into twelve 4 ounce balls. Turn each ball into a patty by using the STUFF side of the burger press to push it down.

> Combine all Spicy Mayo ingredients into a bowl and smash with a fork

> Fill half of the patties with 1 avocado slice and some of the mayo mixture in the center of the patty.

> Place the other patty on top of the stuffed patty.

> Use the SEAL side of the Burger Press to keep the two patties in place. Close the press firmly, which will seal the patties together. Release the press.

> Put the patties on the grill and cook for 6 minutes on each side.

> Serve on a bun and top with mayo, avocado, kale, arugula, and romaine.

VEGGIE MANIA

This recipe showcases squash and elevates it from a lowly side dish to a main dish. Here squash is the star of the show and once you try it, you will understand why.

Prep Time: 15 Minutes

Cook Time: 1 Hour

Servings: 4

INGREDIENTS:

1 delicata squash, halved lengthwise and seeded

1 tablespoon olive oil (optional)

salt and ground black pepper to taste

2 tablespoons butter

1 shallot, minced

1 clove garlic, minced

6 sun-dried tomatoes, chopped

1 cup bread crumbs, or more if needed

1 egg, beaten

1/4 cup grated Parmesan cheese

1/4 cup vegetable oil, or as needed

DIRECTIONS:

> Put squash on a baking sheet, sprinkle with olive oil and cook for 40 minutes at 470 degrees. Cut into cubes when it cools down.

> Cook and stir shallots and garlic in butter for 10 minutes. Stir in sun-dried tomatoes and cook for 3 more minutes.

> Add the squash to this mixture, mash and let cool down.

> Combine bread crumbs, the egg and parmesan cheese into the squash mixture.

> Form the squash mixture into four 4 ounce balls. Turn each ball into a patty by using the STUFF side of the burger press to push it down.

> Fry in a nonstick pan for four to five minutes on each side.

> Serve on a whole wheat bun and choose the condiments that would work best for this burger.

HONEY GLAZED AND AMAZED

Honey makes everything sweet and this burger is no exception. The honey glaze in the burger counteracts with the garlic and the cheese, but something about it makes it work wonders.

Prep Time: 5 Minutes

Cook Time: 20 Minutes

Servings: 2

INGREDIENTS:

4 full onions, center sliced

1 tablespoon honey

1 teaspoon garlic

1/4 teaspoon salt

1/8 teaspoon pepper

1 pound lean ground beef

1/4 cup finely shredded cheddar cheese

2 hamburger buns split

Lettuce leaves and tomato slices, optional

DIRECTIONS:

> Combine the garlic, salt and pepper in a bowl. Mix these ingredients with the beef.

> Form the ground beef mixture into four 4 ounce balls. Turn each ball into a patty by using the STUFF side of the burger press to push it down.
> Fill half of the patties with a handful of cheese and one full onion in the center of each patty.
> Place the other patty on top of the stuffed patty.
> Use the SEAL side of the Burger Press to keep the two patties in place. Close the press firmly, which will seal the patties together. Release the press.
> Brush the patty with honey on each side.
> Put the patties on the grill and cook for 6 minutes on each side. Add some more honey

Serve on buns with lettuce and tomato if desired.

VEGGIES "R" US

Edamame stuffed wasabi cheese in a burger will tease your taste buds and have you begging for more. Rich with vegetables, you will rave about its potato goodness.

Prep Time: 10 Minutes
Cook Time: 35 Minutes
Servings: 6

INGREDIENTS:
1 large sweet potato, diced
2 tbsp. extra virgin olive oil
3 large portabella mushroom caps, chopped
3 scallions, sliced
1 large zucchini squash, grated
2 large carrots, grated
1 cup rolled oats
½ cup frozen shelled edamame, thawed
2 tbsp. arrowroot powder (corn or potato starch)
2 tbsp. mustard
Juice of 1 lime
½ tsp. salt
1 Oz Sincerely Brigitte Wasabi Cheese per burger
6 big tomatoes, sliced in half (serve as a bun)

DIRECTIONS:

> Cook sweet potatoes in a pot and bring to a boil, for ten minutes. Smash with fork

> Combine scallions mushrooms, carrots, zucchini and salt and cook for 8 minutes in a skillet.

> Add oats, mashed sweet potatoes, edamame powder, mustard, lime and salt to the mix. Blend it until it mixes together

> Form the mixture into twelve 4 ounce balls. Turn each ball into a patty by using the STUFF side of the burger press to push it down.

> Fill half of the patties with a piece of cheese that has been cut up into three pieces

> Place the other patty on top of the stuffed patty.

> Use the SEAL side of the Burger Press to keep the two patties in place. Close the press firmly, which will seal the patties together. Release the press.

> Cook on the grill for 6 minutes per side.

> Serve on a wheat bun

THE GARDEN GORILLA

This is the greatest burger for potato lovers. It is all of your favorite ingredients in a bun.

Prep Time: 5 Minutes
Cook Time: 22 Minutes
Servings: 6

INGREDIENTS:
1 cup canned black beans
1 grated carrot
½ diced medium onion
3 grated medium sized potatoes
4 chopped green onions
1 cup frozen or canned corn kernels
½ teaspoon garlic salt

DIRECTIONS:
> Drain the beans from the can and mash them.
> Combine all of the ingredients together in a bowl.
> Put the patties on the grill and cook for 3 minutes on each side
> Serve on a bun with ketchup, lettuce and tomato.

THE MAGIC MUSHROOMED

If you love mushrooms, then this is the burger for you. In this recipe, we cook the mushrooms right inside the burger

Prep Time: 10 Minutes

Cook Time: 40 Minutes

Servings: 8

INGREDIENTS:

1 ½ cups sliced onions

8 ounces mushrooms

1 tablespoon olive oil

2 tablespoons snipped fresh parsley

4 pounds ground beef

1/3 cup Worcestershire sauce

4 minced garlic cloves

1 ½ teaspoons salt

1 teaspoon fine ground pepper

16 sliced Applewood smoked bacon

8 slices Swiss, provolone and Colby Jack Cheese

8 Kaiser Rolls toasted

Tomato slices

DIRECTIONS:

❯   Place the onions and mushrooms in a pan and cook for 20 minutes. Add the parsley and set to the side to cool.

> Combine the beef, Worcestershire, garlic, salt and pepper in a bowl.
> Form the ground beef mixture into sixteen 4 ounce balls. Turn each ball into a patty by using the STUFF side of the burger press to push it down.
> Fill half of the patties with the onion mushroom filling in the center of each patty.
> Place the other patty on top of the stuffed patty.
> Use the SEAL side of the Burger Press to keep the two patties in place. Close the press firmly, which will seal the patties together. Release the press.
> Place onions in a pan and cook for 4 minutes with olive oil and the rest of the salt and pepper.
> Put the patties on the grill and cook for 6 minutes on each side.
> Serve with cheese and tomato slices.

THE "G" SPOT (GREEN)

The great thing about tofu is that it tastes like what you marinate or cook it in. This miso glazed protein burger is not only healthy, but it's flavorful and the lettuce wrap adds a crunch that you would be missing if you used an ordinary bun.

Prep Time: 5 Minutes

Cook Time: 18 Minutes

Servings: 6

INGREDIENTS:
1 (14 ounce) packaged tofu

1 pound ground beef

½ cup shiitake mushrooms, sliced

2 tbsp. miso paste

1 egg, lightly beaten

1 tsp. salt

1 tsp. ground black pepper

¼ cup mirin (Japanese sweet wine)

1 teaspoon garlic paste

¼ teaspoon fresh ginger root, minced

1 tbsp. vegetable oil

DIRECTIONS:
> Press the tofu down until it is flattened. Discard the liquid and cut it into small pieces.

> Combine ground beef, tofu, mushrooms, miso, egg, salt, pepper and nutmeg in a bowl
> To form the burgers, combine the egg and bread crumbs into a bowl
> Form the mixture into six 4 ounce balls. Turn each ball into a patty by using the STUFF side of the burger press to push it down.
> Stir in the sauces and the rest of the spices and put aside
> Cook the burgers on the grill for about 8 minutes on each side
> Pour the sauce on the burgers when they are almost done cooking to add the glaze
> Serve over lettuce leaves, or seaweed.

CULINARY ORGASM

This will have your taste buds screaming more please! It pairs the delicious flavors of crab and beef. Pair with a wine cooler, curl up with a book and chow down.

Prep Time: 5 Minutes
Cook Time: 20 Minutes
Servings: 6

INGREDIENTS:

3 pounds certified Angus Beef ground chuck
1 teaspoon horseradish
3 teaspoons Old Bay seasoning
1 1/3 bread crumbs
1 cup lump crabmeat
2 tablespoons chopped fresh cilantro
2 tablespoons finely chopped green onions
2 tablespoons mayonnaise
½ teaspoon Dijon mustard
1 teaspoon lemon zest
½ teaspoon ground ginger
6 buns

DIRECTIONS:

> Combine the ground beef and 2 teaspoons Old Bay Seasoning into a bowl.

> Combine the cilantro, green onions, mayonnaise, lemon zest and ginger in a separate bowl.

> Combine the crabmeat, bread crumbs, cilantro, green onion, mayonnaise, mustard, lemon zest; ground ginger and remaining Old Bay Seasoning into a bowl.

> Form the ground beef mixture into twelve 4 ounce balls. Turn each ball into a patty by using the STUFF side of the burger press to push it down.

> Fill half of the patties with a little bit of crab.

> Place the other patty on top of the stuffed patty.

> Use the SEAL side of the Burger Press to keep the two patties in place. Close the press firmly, which will seal the patties together. Release the press.

> Put the patties on the grill and cook for 6 minutes on each side.

> Serve: with spreading horse radish on the bottom bun, top with the salad mixture, the patty, Dijon mustard and the top part of the bun.

DOUBLE DECKER TURKEYZILLA CLUB BURGER

Who doesn't love a patty melt or a club? This burger has both. With ground turkey, deli ham and bacon, this burger is full of protein and so much more.

Prep Time:
Cook Time:
Servings:

INGREDIENTS:
1 cup Thousand Island dressing
1 whole avocado, sliced and pitted
8 slices of bacon
1 tomato, sliced
8 pieces of spinach lettuce
2 pounds of ground turkey
8 slices of black forest ham, deli sliced
8 pieces of cheddar cheese
8 slices of sourdough, toasted and cut in half

DIRECTIONS:
> Cook the bacon in a skillet for 12 minutes until crispy.
> Form the ground turkey into eight 4 ounce balls. Create each ball into a patty by using the STUFF side of the burger press to push it down.
> Fill 1 of the patties with a slice of cheese and 1 piece of ham.

> Place the other patty on top of the other patty
> Use the SEAL side of the Burger Press to keep the two patties in place. Close the press firmly, which will seal the patties together. Release the press.
> Put the patties on the grill and cook for 6 minutes on each side
> Serve 1 piece of bread, spread with dressing, add spinach, tomato, 2 slices of bacon, burger patty, 1 more slice of bread, 1 piece of ham, and a slice of cheese, avocado and top with the last slice of bread. Repeat for the other burgers, creating four in total.

BLING BLING BURGER

The tastes of this burger will seduce you and takes you to the romantic city of Paris. We have paired foie gras, with truffles and rib meat for a burger recipe that you would have never thought of in your wildest dreams.

Prep Time: 5 Minutes
Cook Time: 20 Minutes
Serving: 1

INGREDIENTS:

18 paper-thin slices preserved black truffle
¼ cup shredded red wine-braised short rib meat plus 2 tbsp. reserved braising juices
1 ounce foie gras
1 tbsp. carrot, minced
1 tbsp. celery, minced
1 tbsp. white onion, minced
6 ounces ground sirloin
4 tsp. horseradish mayonnaise
1 parmesan Kaiser roll, sliced and toasted
6 red onion strings, sliced
2 thin slices of tomato
1/3 cup packed frisee, cleaned and dried
½ tbsp. unsalted butter
6 pieces tomato confit

DIRECTIONS:

> Combine truffle slices with the short rib meat in a small bowl.
> Cook the foie gras for four minutes in a pan until browned
> Reduce the heat and add carrots, celery, white onion and salt and pepper to the pan. Cook for 1 minute.
> Add the rib mixture and braising juices and combine with the rest of the mixture in the pan.
> Form the ground rib mixture into two 4 ounce balls.
> Fill the patty with the foie gras in the center.
> Place the other patty on top of the stuffed patty.
> Use the SEAL side of the Burger Press to keep the two patties in place. Close the press firmly, which will seal the patties together. Release the press.
> Put the patties on the grill and cook for 8 minutes on each side.
> Serve: spread mayonnaise on the bottom bun, red onion, tomato slices, frisee and the burger patty. Top with butter and tomato confit. Spread the remaining mayonnaise on the top bun.

THE JACK RABBIT BURGER

Chicken, BBQ sauce and blue cheese dressing? What's not to like. It's like a hot wing, but in a bun. This burger will make your taste buds soar with pleasure.

Prep Time: 5 Minutes

Cook Time: 25 Minutes

Servings: 5

INGREDIENTS:

¼ cup buffalo wing sauce

2 tablespoons Kraft original Barbeque Sauce

2 pound ground chicken

1 package SHAKE 'N BAKE Extra Crispy Seasoned Coating Mix

1 egg

4 hamburger buns

4 leaf lettuce leaves

¼ cup KRAFT Blue Cheese Dressing

2 stalks celery, cut into sticks

2 carrots cut into sticks

DIRECTIONS:

> Combine the buffalo wing sauce and blue cheese dressing into a bowl.

> Combine the ground chicken, Shake 'N Bake and egg into a bowl.

> Form the ground chicken mixture into eight 4 ounce balls. Turn each ball into a patty by using the STUFF side of the burger press to push it down.
> Brush one side of the burger with the BBQ sauce
> Put the patties on the grill and cook for 6 minutes on each side. Spread the patty with the sauce mixture the last two minutes it is cooking.
> Serve on a bun and spread the sun and top with lettuce. Serve the celery, carrots and remaining blue cheese dressing on the side.

CHEEZY GORDO GARLIC LOVERS BURGER

Want to try something new? Think out of the box a little bit? You will love the softness of the French bread paired with the ooziness of the cheese and the way that the garlic stands out.

Prep Time: 5 Minutes

Cook Time: 20 Minutes

Servings: 4

INGREDIENTS:

3 cups sliced onion

4 teaspoons olive oil

1/4 teaspoon salt

1/4 teaspoon coarsely ground pepper

2 pound lean ground beef

2 tablespoons Worcestershire sauce

1/2 teaspoon coarse ground pepper

2 cloves garlic, minced

3/4 cup shredded Swiss cheese (3 oz.)

4 3/4-inch-thick diagonally cut French bread slices

1 tablespoon olive oil

DIRECTIONS:

> Place the onions and oil in a pan and cook for 10 minutes. Add salt and pepper and set to the side to stay warm.

> Combine the beef, Worcestershire, ½ tsp. pepper and garlic in a bowl.

> Form the ground beef mixture into eight 4 ounce balls. Turn each ball into a patty by using the STUFF side of the burger press to push it down.
> Fill half of the patties with ¼ of the cheese in the center of each patty.
> Place the other patty on top of the stuffed patty.
> Use the SEAL side of the Burger Press to keep the two patties in place. Close the press firmly, which will seal the patties together. Release the press.
> Place onions in a pan and cook for 4 minutes with olive oil and the rest of the salt and pepper.
> Put the patties on the grill and cook for 6 minutes on each side.
> Brush the bread with some olive oil and set on the grill for 3 minutes
> Serve: on a toasted piece of bread and top with the onion mix, the burger and top with another piece of bread.

VEGAN MEDITERRANEAN DELIGHT

This burger has all different types of herbs and spices that boost its flavor. Chickpeas stuffed in pita bread. Sounds like a great choice for an evening meal.

Prep Time: 20 Minutes

Cook Time: 1 hour

Servings: 8

INGREDIENTS:

2 tbsp. plus 1 tsp. olive oil

2 cups baby spinach

1 large yellow onion, chopped

4 cloves garlic, minced

1 ¼ cups vegan vegetable broth

½ cup cracked freekeh

1 can chickpeas, drained, rinsed and patted dry

½ cup panko bread crumbs

¼ cup chopped parsley

¼ cup sunflower seeds, chopped

2 tbsp. fresh lemon juice

1 ½ tsp. grated lemon zest

1 ½ tsp. ground cumin

1 tsp. ground coriander

1 tsp. salt & 1 tsp. pepper

1 vegan egg, beaten

2 tbsp. canola oil
Small pita breads, for serving

Tzatziki:

1 cup vegan plain yogurt
¼ cup finely shredded cucumber
1 clove garlic, minced
2 tsp. fresh minced dill
Salt and pepper

Tomato Salad:

2 tomatoes, chopped
¼ cup red onion, chopped
2 tbsp. parsley, chopped
½ of a lemon juice
Salt and pepper

DIRECTIONS:

> Cook the spinach in a skillet until wilted for 2 minutes. Remove. Let cool and then chop.
> Add the onion in the pan for 5 minutes to brown. Then add the garlic, broth and freekeh and boil. Cook for 20 minutes until the freekeh is soft.
> Combine the spinach, freekah, chickpeas, panko, parsley, sunflower seeds, lemon juice, zest, cumin and coriander to a bowl. Mash until the chickpeas are no longer chunky. Add the egg and stir. Let the mixture cool for an hour.

> To form the burgers, combine the egg and bread crumbs into a bowl.
> Form the mixture into eight 4 ounce balls. Turn each ball into a patty by using the STUFF side of the burger press to push it down.
> On the grill cook the burgers for 6 minutes on each side.
> Serve: on warm pita bread with the Tzatziki sauce and tomato salad
> Tzatziki Sauce: Combine all of the ingredients together.
> Tomato Salad: Combine all of the ingredients together.

MAC & CHEESE STUFFED BURGER

Do you remember when you used to dip French fries in your ice cream or stuff your burger with French fries? That was comfort food at its finest. Stuff your burger with mac and cheese and feel like a kid again.

Prep Time: 5 Minutes

Cook Time: 20 Minutes

Servings: 6

INGREDIENTS:

½ tbsp. butter

½ tbsp. flour

¼ cup milk

¼ tsp. salt

1/8 tsp. black pepper

½ cup grated medium Cheddar cheese

½ cup cooked macaroni noodles

2 lbs. ground chuck

Vegetable oil, for brushing on the grill rack

6 potato hamburger buns, split

6 tbsp. ketchup

6 tsp. yellow mustard

DIRECTIONS:

> **Macaroni and Cheese:** Add saucepan to the grill and melt butter and flour. Gradually pour in the milk. Remember to season with the salt

and pepper. Add the shredded cheese, macaroni noodles and set aside.

> **Burgers:** Combine the ground chuck into a bowl with salt and pepper. Shape the mixture into 12 patties.
> Form the ground chuck into eight 12 ounce balls. Create each ball into a patty by using the STUFF side of the burger press to push it down.
> Fill 1 of the patties with macaroni and cheese, spread evenly.
> Place the other patty on top of the other patty
> Use the SEAL side of the Burger Press to keep the two patties in place. Close the press firmly, which will seal the patties together. Release the press.
> Put the patties on the grill and cook for 6 minutes on each side
> Grill over medium heat for 6 minutes on each side.
> Spread mustard and ketchup sauce on a bun and top with lettuce and tomato

SUPER BIG "BAD ASS" STUFFED BLUE CHEESE BURGER

These burgers might seem simple, but there is nothing simple about the tanginess of the blue cheese, which pairs perfectly with the onion. It is a match made in heaven.

Prep Time: 5 Minutes
Cook Time: 40 Minutes
Servings: 4

INGREDIENTS:
1 pound lean ground beef
1/2 teaspoon Worcestershire sauce
1 teaspoon dried parsley
Salt and black pepper to taste
1 cup Roquefort or other blue cheese, crumbled
4 Kaiser Rolls, split and heated
4 slices onion, or to taste
4 lettuce leaves
4 slices tomato

DIRECTIONS
> Place the onions and mushrooms in a pan and cook for 20 minutes. Add the parsley and set to the side to cool.
> Combine the beef, Worcestershire, parsley, salt and pepper in a bowl.

> Form the ground beef mixture into four 4 ounce balls. Create each ball into a patty by using the STUFF side of the burger press to push it down.
> Fill 1 of the patties with a ¼ cup of Roquefort cheese in the center of each patty.
> Place the other patty on top of the other patty
> Use the SEAL side of the Burger Press to keep the two patties in place. Close the press firmly, which will seal the patties together. Release the press.
> Place onions in a pan and cook for 4 minutes with olive oil and the rest of the salt and pepper.
> Put the patties on the grill and cook for 6 minutes on each side.
> Serve on a heated Kaiser roll with sliced onion, lettuce, and tomato on the side.

MEXICAN POLLO SOMBRERRO BURGER

This burger will make you feel like a party in your mouth. Fresh Pico di Gallo, Jalapenos and cilantro will have you forgetting that you aren't eating a taco.

Prep Time: 5 Minutes
Cook Time: 20 Minutes
Servings: 4

INGREDIENTS:
1½ lbs. lean ground chicken
Kosher Salt
Fresh Ground Pepper
½ cup Pico Di Gallo
1 cup chopped jalapenos
1 cup shredded Mexican Blend Cheese
Fresh Cilantro

DIRECTIONS:
> Mix the ground chicken, salt, pepper and Pico di Gallo into a bowl.
> Form the ground chicken mixture into eight 4 ounce balls. Create each ball into a patty by using the STUFF side of the burger press to push it down.
> Fill 1 of the patties with Pico di Gallo, jalapenos, and cheese blend.
> Place the other patty on top of the other patty

> Use the SEAL side of the Burger Press to keep the two patties in place. Close the press firmly, which will seal the patties together. Release the press.
> Put the patties on the grill and cook for 6 minutes on each side.
> Serve: with the remaining Pico di Gallo on a roll and top with fresh cilantro.

BACON DOUBLE WRAPPED STUFFED OSTRICH BURGER

Dying to try something new, but not too new? Try an ostrich burger. It's a taste of the outback with a little slice of the American pie.

Prep Time: 5 Minutes
Cook Time: 20 minutes
Servings: 6

INGREDIENTS:
1 ½ pounds ground ostrich
2 teaspoons chopped garlic
1 teaspoon grated ginger
2 teaspoons chopped chills
1 packet of chopped flat leaf parsley
Sea Salt
Fresh ground pepper
4 teaspoons onion marmalade
1 pound bacon
4 hamburger buns, toasted

DESCRIPTION:
❯ Combine the ground ostrich, garlic, ginger, chili's, parsley, salt and pepper together in a bowl.

> Form the ground beef mixture into six 4 ounce balls. Create each ball into a patty by using the STUFF side of the burger press to push it down.
> Fill 1 of the patties with the place the onion marmalade in the center of each patty and wrap the bacon around each patty.
> Place the other patty on top of the other patty
> Use the SEAL side of the Burger Press to keep the two patties in place. Close the press firmly, which will seal the patties together. Release the press.
> Put the patties on the grill and cook for 6 minutes on each side.
> Serve on a bun with lettuce, tomato.

DOUBLE STUFFED CHEESE ALPHA BURGER

Everything is always better with beer or stout for that matter. This Irish stout burger is marinated in stout, Worcestershire sauce and shallots. It will make you feel like a regular Dubliner.

Prep Time:
Cook Time:
Servings: 4

INGREDIENTS:

1 ½ pounds ground pork
¼ cup shallots, chopped
2 tsp. Worcestershire sauce
½ tsp. salt
¼ pepper
½ cup shredded Dubliner cheese with Irish Stout
4 hamburger rolls, split
4 lettuce leaves
4 tomato slices
4 tsp. mayonnaise

DIRECTIONS:

❯ Combine pork, shallots, Worcestershire sauce, salt and pepper into a bowl.

> Form the ground pork into eight 4 ounce balls. Create each ball into a patty by using the STUFF side of the burger press to push it down.
> Fill 1 of the patties with 2 tbsp. of cheese.
> Place the other patty on top of the other patty
> Use the SEAL side of the Burger Press to keep the two patties in place. Close the press firmly, which will seal the patties together. Release the press.
> Put the patties on the grill and cook for 6 minutes on each side
> Serve: place 1 lettuce leaf, 1 tomato slice, and 1 burger. Spread the top roll with mayonnaise and put on top of the patty.

ONION PEPPER MARYLAND CRAB CAKE BURGER

Did you ever have a hard time making up your mind on eating seafood or a burger? Well, this is seafood in place of a burger. Don't let it fool you though, once you bite into this burger, it might become your go to every time.

Prep Time: 5 Minutes

Cook Time: 25 Minutes

Servings: 6

INGREDIENTS:

Dressing:

¼ cup mayonnaise

2 thinly sliced green onions

2 tablespoons minced drained roasted red pepper from jar

1 tablespoon fresh lemon juice

1 tablespoon ketchup

1 tablespoon hot chili sauce

1 tablespoon hot chili sauce

¼ teaspoon finely grated lemon peel

Burgers:

¼ cup mayonnaise

1 large egg

2 tablespoons ketchup

1 teaspoon finely grated lemon peel

1 teaspoon hot chili sauce

½ teaspoon coarse kosher salt

2 tablespoons minced drained roasted red pepper from jar

1 thinly sliced green onion

1 pound fresh lump crabmeat

1 ¾ cups panko

3 ciabatta rolls, halved

2 tablespoons butter

6 crisp heart of romaine lettuce leaves

DIRECTIONS:
Dressing:
> Combine all ingredients into a bowl and season with salt and pepper.

Burgers:
> Combine the first 8 ingredients into a bowl. Add in the crab meat and the panko.
> Form the crab mixture into six 4 ounce balls. Create each ball into a patty by using the STUFF side of the burger press to push it down.
> Put the patties on the grill and cook for 6 minutes on each side
> Spread butter on the rolls and place on the grill mat for 2 minutes.
> Place the burger on the grill mat and grill over medium heat for 5 minutes on each side.
> Serve on a bun and top with lettuce. Spread dressing on the burger and bun for flavor.

STUFFED LOBSTER INFUZED CRAB ROLL

The taste of Maine on a burger. Stuffing lobster with crab is a great way for us to celebrate this East Coast favorite. Pair it with a great wine cooler and you got yourself one memorable meal.

Prep Time:

Cook Time:

Servings:

INGREDIENTS:
1 pound lumped crab meat
4 cups cooked lobster meat, cubed
1 ¾ panko bread crumbs
1 egg, beaten
½ cup mayonnaise
¼ cup green onions, chopped
1 tbsp. celery, chopped
1 tbsp. fresh lemon juice
½ teaspoon salt
Dash hot sauce
Sliced French bread, toasted and buttered

DESCRIPTION:
> Combine the green onions, celery, lemon juice, salt and hot sauce into a bowl. Mix and toss. Set aside

> To form the burgers, combine the egg and bread crumbs into a bowl. Add the lobster meat and mix together.
> Form the lobster mixture into eight 4 ounce balls. Create each ball into a patty by using the STUFF side of the burger press to push it down.
> Fill 1 of the patties with the crab meat
> Place the other patty on top of the other patty
> Use the SEAL side of the Burger Press to keep the two patties in place. Close the press firmly, which will seal the patties together. Release the press.
> Fry in a pan for 6 minutes on each side.
> Serve: bottom of French bread add mayonnaise, place a spoonful of salad mixture, add the patty and top with the remaining bun. Serve with a wine cooler.

BIG BISON NACHO EXTREME BURGER

The Ground Turkey Nacho Burger combines both Nachos and a Burger in one sitting. The crunchiness of the potato chips makes for a delicious meal that you can still eat with your hands.

Prep Time: 5 Minutes

Cook Time: 20 Minutes

Servings: 4

INGREDIENTS:

1 cup heavy cream

2 garlic cloves, grated

2 tbsp. grated parmigiana Reggiano cheese

1 ½ pounds ground bison

1 tbsp. Worcestershire sauce

Salt and pepper

2 tbsp. onion, grated

2 tbsp. parsley, chopped

2 tbsp. butter

2 tbsp. hot sauce

4 tortillas, heated and toasted

A bag of thick-cut potato chips

½ cup blue cheese crumbles

Chopped chives

DIRECTIONS:

❯ Combine cream and garlic in a pan and bring to a boil. Cook for 8 minutes while stirring in the cheese

❯ Combine the bison, Worcestershire, salt, pepper, onion and parsley together.

❯ Form the mixture into four 4 ounce balls. Create each ball into a patty by using the STUFF side of the burger press to push it down.

❯ Cook on the grill for 6 minutes on each side. Pour the hot sauce and the butter onto the burgers while cooking.

❯ Serve: Place the burger on the bottom bun. Top with the potato chips, cream sauce, blue cheese and green onions.

SUPER SALAMI GLAZED STALLION BURGER

Italian dressing is great for more than salads. This recipe stuffs salami with artichoke hearts and marinates the burger in Italian dressing. Then we finish it off with capers, tomatoes and Peppercini's and use breadsticks as our bun. Enjoy.

Prep Time: 5 Minutes

Cook Time: 20 Minutes

Servings: 4

INGREDIENTS:
1½ lbs. lean ground salami

Kosher Salt

Fresh Ground Pepper

½ cup Italian dressing

1 teaspoon garlic powder

½ teaspoon dried basil or oregano, crushed

4 slices Mozzarella and Provolone

8 artichoke hearts

Capers, for taste

1 tomato, sliced

Peppercini's Diced

4 Romaine hearts

16 breadsticks

DIRECTIONS:

❯ Mix the ground salami, salt, pepper, ¼ Italian dressing, and garlic powder into a bowl.

❯ Form the ground salami into eight 4 ounce balls. Create each ball into a patty by using the STUFF side of the burger press to push it down.

❯ Fill 1 of the patties with 2 artichoke hearts and one piece of provolone and mozzarella cheese.

❯ Place the other patty on top of the other patty

❯ Use the SEAL side of the Burger Press to keep the two patties in place. Close the press firmly, which will seal the patties together. Release the press.

❯ Brush the patties with Italian dressing on both sides

❯ Put the patties on the grill and cook for 6 minutes on each side. Put some more of the dressing on the patties before they are done cooking.

❯ Serve: Dust two breadsticks with the dressing, and top with capers, Peppercini's, the patty and a romaine heart. Top with 2 more breadsticks to finish the burger.

SPICY JALAPEÑO APPLE SAUSAGE & CHICKEN BURGER

This burger makes poultry the star. Here we combine Turkey and Chicken sausage for a flavor that you won't want to miss. This is not a contest to see which one is sweeter or moister. Here we are paring them as two fowl friends who are equally tasty and full of great flavors.

Prep Time: 5 Minutes
Cook Time: 20 Minutes
Servings: 4

INGREDIENTS:
1 pound ground turkey
1 pound ground apple smoked chicken sausage
Kosher Salt
Fresh Ground Pepper
½ cup feta cheese
½ cup fresh spinach, chopped
4 servings of hamburger buns
Ketchup, for taste
Mustard, for taste

DIRECTIONS:
> Mix the ground chicken and ground turkey with the salt and pepper

> Form the ground chicken mixture and the ground turkey mixture into eight 4 ounce balls. Create each ball into a patty by using the STUFF side of the burger press to push it down.
> Fill 1 of the chicken patties with ¼ of the feta cheese and ¼ of the spinach.
> Place the other patty on top of the other patty
> Use the SEAL side of the Burger Press to keep the two patties in place. Close the press firmly, which will seal the patties together. Release the press.
> Put the patties on the grill and cook for 6 minutes on each side.
> Serve on the bun with ketchup and mustard

MEAT MARINADES FOR BURGERS

These two marinades will due for any of these recipes in the book. These are the two favorites that are my "go-to's" for any barbecue or cooking occasion.

MEAT HEAT INFUZION

INGREDIENTS:

1/2 cup Italian dressing

1/2 teaspoon lemon juice

1/2 teaspoon minced garlic

1/2 teaspoon Tabasco sauce

1/2 teaspoon dried basil

1/2 teaspoon Cayenne pepper

DIRECTIONS:

> Combine all of these ingredients together in a blender for best results!

CAJUN KICKER

INSTRUCTIONS:

1/3 cup soy sauce

1/2 cup red wine

2 tablespoons Cajun seasoning

2 tablespoons minced garlic

2 tablespoons brown sugar

1/2 teaspoon cinnamon

1 tablespoon tomato paste

1 teaspoon fresh ground pepper

1 splash of lemon juice

DIRECTIONS:

> Combine all of these ingredients together in a blender for best results!

NEXT ON THE LIST!

HERE'S WHAT YOU DO NOW...

If you were pleased with our book then PLEASE LEAVE US A COOL REVIEW ON AMAZON **where you purchased this book!** In the world of an author who writes books independently, your reviews are not only touching but important so that we know you like the material we have prepared for "you" our audience! So, leave us a review...we would love to see that you enjoyed our book!

If for any reason that you were less than happy with your experience then send me an email at **Info@RecipeNerds.com** and let me know how we can better your experience. We always come out with a few volumes of our books and will possibly be able to address some of your concerns. Do keep in mind that we strive to do our best to give you the highest quality of what "we the independent authors" pour our heart and tears into.

I am very happy to create new and exciting recipes and do appreciate your purchase. I thank you for your many great reviews and comments! With a warm heart! ~A.J. Luigi "Professional Loving Chef"

YOURS TO KEEP!

12 Steps to Making the Perfect Stuffed or Unstuffed Burgers with your STUFFED Burger Press! This quick start guide will show you the way to get the **BEST Burgers made fast!** This **QUICK STEP GUIDE** will make you a pro at stuffing those burgers! Simply click the button below! Enjoy your Monster Burgers! GET YOURS NOW!

http://eepurl.com/dt_9IX

ABOUT THE AUTHOR

Rex Houston is a real Cowboy at heart! Growing up in the mid-west, developing a love for that down-home cooking, he has made a Professional career as a Gourmet Chef. This self-taught master chef is true to his cooking and has well over 15 years of experience in this game! He is best known for some of his award winning mid-western chili! Better than mom used to make! Rex loves making special recipes just for you! These recipes in this book are some of his very own personal favorites, and some of the best in the west, that he has shared with you. So, fasten your seatbelt and I hope you enjoy these recipes that we have mapped out for you! Straight from me, to you! And remember, leave me a cool review on Amazon!

Hope you enjoy!
Tex-Rex!

PERSONAL BURGER RECIPES & NOTES:

Create your very own "Marvelous Masterpieces". Log them in this section. You will be amazed on how many ideas you come up with! **Now get creating!**

Burger Name	Meat	Bun Type	Toppings

Made in the USA
Las Vegas, NV
20 December 2022

63706634R00059